INTO

The Open Economy

Colin R. Turner

Published by Applied Image, October 2016
ISBN: 978-0-9560640-4-2
First edition 2016
Text version 1.2

Edited by Krisztina Paterson and Sarah McIver.

Book news and updates may be found at:
freeworlder.com
facebook.com/intotheopeneconomy

FROM THE SAME AUTHOR:

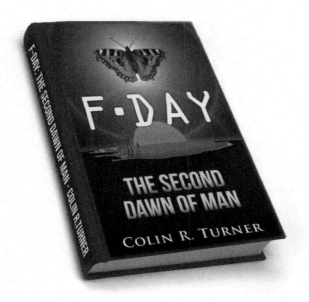

F–DAY: THE SECOND DAWN OF MAN

A FICTIONAL DRAMATISATION OF THE
BIRTH OF AN OPEN ECONOMY

FIVE STAR READER RATED

AVAILABLE NOW ON AMAZON

Life is an open secret.

Everything is available.
Nothing is hidden.

All you need are the eyes to see.

~ OSHO

Contents

An Offer

I offer this book in good faith as a concerned cohabitant of Earth. I believe this makes me equally qualified as any other to present some opinions and options for an alternative society that I feel urgently need to be expressed. But, before we begin:

> ➢ If you're looking for a long complex manifesto of convoluted theories, you're not going to find them here. The ideas expressed here are simple because the solutions I propose are simple.

> ➢ If you're looking for an authoritative document, thick with citations, references, and an author with scholarly accreditations, you're not going to find these here. All the ideas expressed in this book are based on common sense and everyday experience. My only qualification is forty-eight years of life experience, of which the last five, since authoring *The Free World Charter*, have been spent in much contemplation of this topic.

> ➢ Almost nothing in this book is new. The ideas expressed here will almost certainly already be familiar to you. The only thing that's unique is how we are going to apply or combine those ideas.

If you are happy with these 'rules of engagement' and are interested in exploring some amazing possibilities for our future, then please follow me...

Introduction

The format of this book – like everything else about it – is simple. I present a solution to a problem or an alternative method of achieving something, then why I think it will work. The evidence and references for my claims will (I hope) be self-evident by your *own* experience.

When it comes to learning new information, there is simply no comparison to *experiencing* it. That is why I think this approach will work better in explaining the Open Economy. Rather than wasting my time and yours expanding vast amounts of data, I can show you how it works based on what you *already know*.

Our world view has become suffused with theories. Theories regarding behaviour and economics that I believe are now limiting our range of possibilities.

Let us remember that the fields of economics and human behaviour are based on *observations*. They do not predict the future, nor are they rules that we must obey.

Many of these observation-based theories were made hundreds of years ago. Since then, mechanisation, electricity, computerisation and communications have changed the game on this planet forever. This has given us the potential to radically alter our environment, and thus our behaviour *and* economy.

Our world is constantly changing. And while we may create convincing theories, we are not subject to them.

Your most valuable source of reference is your own life experience and the people around you. Media and prevailing thought present a distorted view of the world. The actions of 'evil' people are given exaggerated importance, but they are *very much the exception to normal behaviour.* The number of truly bad people in the world is actually statistically irrelevant. This is *crucially* important to remember.

Almost every person I can think of – who I've met personally – is a reasonably decent person. Even if they are not always decent with me, I know that they behave decently with the people they *do* care about and understand what it means to do the 'right thing'.

This seems to be the experience of everyone I ask too. The vast majority of people are good. I would like you to apply this outlook when appraising the concepts here. Base your conclusions *only* on the behaviour of people *you know personally*, not from gleaned impressions.

Finally, on the cover of this book I made the rather bold statement: '*How everything you know about the world is about to change*', and you may well be wondering how I can qualify such a remark. Well, I believe I can, because this statement is, in fact, a double-edged sword.

The world you know *is* about to change, whether in general alignment with the principles expressed in this book towards a fairer, sustainable future for all, or continuing blindly on its reckless course toward social decay, violence and environmental catastrophe. It *must* go one way or the other.

I prefer the former option – and the good news is it's something we can all organise with minimal effort. So let's begin.

INTO THE OPEN ECONOMY

The Problem(s)

This is intended to be a book of solutions, so I won't dwell too much on the problems of the world here. Most of them are obvious, but in case you missed any, here they are briefly:

➢ Perpetuation of economic growth – requiring ever more resources – coupled with population expansion on a planet with finite resources.

➢ Relentless and permanent destruction of natural habitat to maintain industry and agriculture, at the expense of biodiversity.

➢ Vast income and social inequality.

➢ Unemployment and the erosion of the labour market through automation and artificial intelligence systems.

➢ Irresponsible behaviour, waste and inefficiency caused through the prioritisation of profit, i.e. what's good for others or the environment is either left to chance or must be enforced through regulation.

➢ Waste of resources and under-achievement through short-sighted production methods, i.e. it's more profitable to sell something inferior repeatedly than to build something that lasts.

> Inter-personal and community disconnection, i.e. trading and competition promote personal isolation.

I should add, these problems are in no particular order. Each is a serious cause for concern on its own.

When you break it down, integral to each one of these problems is our market system, or to be more precise: our primary methods of distributing resources and conducting society, namely: *trade and governance*.

Since most people generally assume that trade is a non-negotiable fact of life, the questions arises: can we improve our trade and government systems to better serve everyone?

While it *is* definitely possible to improve on what we have – and many progressive governments are doing so – these systems are by their very nature limited and inefficient. *We simply can't afford to waste any more time and planet constraining ourselves this way.*

Let me show you what I mean.

The Limitations of Governance

Firstly, you need to see traditional government as really nothing more than an outgrowth of the trading system, whose principal duties are to oversee and regulate the economy.

Imagine for a moment that we had no need for any type of trading economy. No markets, no money, no jobs, wages, bills or taxes. It soon becomes difficult to see what power or purpose any government would have in such a system.

Being itself *part* of the economy, the government is limited by what it can do. We have all heard plenty about cutbacks for state services, the national debt, or the stories of corruption, corporate lobbying and vested interests in undesirable policies. Government – and its individual members – are all very much subject to the economy, and therefore have only very limited control over it.

What it can do is print money, allocate state funding and set interest rates. But, as any economist will tell you, printing money doesn't solve anything. Prices just rise accordingly over time. State spending and interest rates do not control the economy – they are merely *reactions* to it. When the economy is good, the government spends, when the economy is bad, the government cuts back.

Instead of shaping the economy, all the government is really doing is 'housekeeping' the best it can with the fruits of the wider economy on its doorstep.

As to the idea of nations – the centuries-old borders that we define ourselves by – they don't really serve much purpose beyond giving governments a reason to exist. Yes, we need local administration, but this ancient notion of isolated 'nations', restricting the free movement of people and resources in the 21st century is kind of preposterous – and dangerously divisive.

While flag-waving may give some a sense of national pride, it also draws animosity from outsiders. What possible purpose does this divisiveness serve?

When you think about it, we are all born into nations that we had no hand, act or part in creating, so what are we actually proud of? There are many more wholesome things to be proud of, such as your own achievements, or your children, or your team, etc.

You may have noticed that the government is by far the most vocal agency in promoting patriotism. I guess as long as people feel they are part of a 'country', then they will more readily accept the legitimacy of government. But consider the people you know. How many of them really care about borders? To most ordinary people, borders are nothing more than an inconvenience while travelling.

And what about law? Isn't that an important function of government?

Well, first ask yourself this: why do we have laws in the first place? Because some people do bad things. So, *why* do some people do bad things? *That* is the question an intelligent species must be asking itself, rather than focusing on endless retribution, justice and writing laws. We should be questioning the reasons for the anti-social behaviour and addressing those problems directly.

If you need a law that tells you what you can and can't do, isn't that really a sign of a system that is not meeting the needs of its people, and a poorly educated population? Shouldn't we aspire to a society where people don't *want or need* to hurt others?

Law is the blunt instrument we use to hide our failure to create a properly educated, nurturing society. Give people what they want and they won't need to steal from you. Reinforce peoples' natural empathy and they will understand why not to hurt you. That won't stop every crime of course – but it should stamp out around 99% of it.

We'll get into law and education in more detail in later chapters.

The Limitations of Trade

Trade is the natural by-product of scarcity. When it is difficult to acquire something you need – whether a thing or a skill – trade usually appears. By and large, it's a good system: I get what I want, you get what you want, and everyone goes home happy. What's wrong with that?

Well, take a look around you and you will quickly see that this 'textbook' version of trade doesn't travel very well outside the textbook. Valuable resources are monopolised; motivation for gain destroys the environment; monetary wealth is heavily concentrated; the ability to sell your labour and skills for a fair price is rapidly diminished by technical advances, rendering trade ever more difficult.

The fact is, any free market trading and private property system will *always* lead to a concentration of wealth and power. Why? The reasons are tragically simple: 1) some people are just better at making deals, and 2) it's much easier to *increase existing* wealth than it is to create new wealth, e.g. you can promote your services and skills more effectively, hire skilled people to help you, and ride out more mistakes along the way.

Wealth concentration is a *fundamental inevitability* of a

market trading and ownership system. It creates a one-way flow, gradually funnelling wealth upwards.

It's important to note that any system that operates on scarcity will always incentivise greedy, self-interested behaviour. It's perfectly natural to want to hoard things that are scarce. Whether you are hoping for a second piece of bread, or for a second speedboat, the thought process is the same: "If it's hard to get, I want more." Add time to this scarcity-based thinking, and, well, you get where we are today – half of the world's combined wealth in the hands of less than a hundred people.[1]

Even if all this were not the case, there is a second reason why trade is limited. Technology.

Our technology has reached a stage now where it is incredibly easy to produce the things we need compared to, say, a hundred years ago. This is great news, but it means that we are completely eroding the labour market too. Once a technology exists to replace a human job, then that happens immediately, and that job never comes back.

As more and more people are displaced through technology, the higher unemployment grows, the less purchasing power they have, the more dysfunctional the system becomes.

Let's be clear: without jobs, there is *no economy*, and

---

1   According to a 2016 Oxfam Davos report *The Economy of the 1%*, half of the world's wealth is now in the hands of 62 individuals.

today our jobs *are continually* being lost to technology.

So, our perfect textbook trading system has become stuck. The only reason it still operates at all is because of credit. As more wealth is funnelled upwards – never to return – governments and banks continually release lines of credit to keep the system flowing. This is the world we live in today: economies buoyed up entirely by credit. Or, to put it bluntly: *nothing whatsoever.*

But it's not just nothing either. In economic terms, these are *debts on our children's future* that are accruing interest minute-by-minute. If we never changed the rules, what sort of indentured future is that to leave behind?

This credit stream, being created now by commercial banks[2], is the main source of all new money entering the economy – which presents a paradox: how do you pay interest on a loan if the money to pay that interest *doesn't even exist*?

The only possible way is through another debt, thus creating a continual cycle of debt, inflation and increased taxation. This is clearly an unrealistic and unsustainable state of affairs.

---

2   Commercial banks really do create the vast majority of new money through making loans. Google 'money creation in the modern economy'

Disconnection

One of the most damaging side effects of the market system is how it foments disconnection between us.

Corporate agencies relentlessly promote shame, fear, guilt and competition as a way to get us to buy their products. Their profit-orientated agendas are injected wholesale into society through powerful media tools, detaching us from the true physical, social and emotional costs of their products.

We see items advertised for bargain prices, but we seldom think about – or are ever shown – what corners were cut to make those bargains possible. Most 'bargains' are usually achieved through either human exploitation or irresponsible resource extraction.

This overriding profit imperative has created a monster – an entire consumer culture, hypnotising us into craving shiny trinkets and gadgets – at the hidden cost of our self-esteem, relationships and natural resources.

Even the use of money itself removes the need for any relations between buyer and seller. You can walk into a store and pay for an apple without saying one word to the fellow human being selling it to you. What amazing insight or opportunity might be missed?

Market forces regularly override conservation when we

find it cheaper to trash something and replace it rather than repair it.

Perhaps the most dangerous of all is how our system disconnects us from our own common or moral sense.

Everything from walking past a fallen trash can (because it's 'not-your-job') to following government orders to kill other people, represents a marker in our disconnection with the world around us and ourselves. We are *disconnected from being personally responsible*.

Have you ever considered the idea that a regular combat soldier obeying orders is actually a murderer? He or she has completely abandoned their own inner sense of morality to inflict death and destruction on others. Isn't it incredible that almost all of society considers this normal? In some cases even honourable?

How much more disconnected can you be to blithely kill other people and feel like you're doing nothing wrong? In any other context we would call that behaviour psychopathic.

Our underlying sense of disconnection from each other and the consequences of our acts – multiplied by seven billion people – is the reason for the chaotic dissonance and mistrust we all feel in the world today.

We have become confused, insecure, and – in spite of all our wonderful communications technology – increasingly isolated.

Two Possible Solutions

In terms of the debt crisis, the apparent solution of the world's finest economic minds is to just kick the problem down the road – because, frankly, they don't know what else to do. Our world's gargantuan multi-trillion dollar global debt remains written across the sky like some giant calculator error. But it's not an error in accounting – it's an error in how we run society.

Our model of trading and governance cannot solve this problem because humanity has simply outgrown that model. So, what's the answer?

Well, one thing is certain. We *will* bring radical change to our society, or radical change *will* come to us, as our problems inch us ever closer to the brink of societal, economic and environmental collapse.

Today, we have the luxury of choice, the opportunity to be objective and choose well for the future. With the right action now, we could create the type of world all our ancestors must have surely dreamed about at one time or another – complete freedom from servitude, from hard labour, and the time to indulge our passions.

But we don't have that much time, and we also have another problem. The people who are generally charged with bringing societal changes are asleep – or arguably drugged – at the wheel.

These people, our politicians – who mean well I hasten to add – simply do not have the sufficient vision or impetus to bring about radical changes. Almost every politician on the planet is already a wealthy individual. That's how they ascended to power. Therefore, the current monetary market system is their *life blood*. For them, to vote against that system would be insane.

So, we have to face the fact that we, the people, must bring change ourselves.

If we are serious about making the radical changes necessary to solve our problems, then there are really only two conceivable approaches.

Solution one

We perform some kind of Frankensteinian economic reset, with global debt forgiveness, fire all the rogue CEOs, bankers and government ministers, break up their corporations and institutions, redistribute global property and wealth, reduce the working week, and bring a fresh mandate for governance directly from the people.

This is the preferred solution for most radical change agents today. Of course, those who control the wealth will almost certainly not agree to this. But, even if they did, or if we somehow forced them, we would just arrive back at the same point as before, due to the same funnelling effect of wealth concentration, the continuing pursuit of profit at the expense of the environment, and the ever dwindling labour market.

In other words, we would have a brand new wealthy elite and all the same basic problems, because that is where we must *always logically arrive within that system*.

The analogy of market capitalism to the Monopoly board game is absolute. Any scarcity-based competition will always gravitate towards there being one winner. Resetting the economy would be just like wiping the Monopoly board clean and starting a new game. As long as you follow the same rules, you will end up with the same result: concentrated wealth and a bunch of losers.

Solution two

We stop, take a step back, and look at the bigger picture. What things are actually important to our lives and our long-term existence on this planet? What are we truly technically capable of? What limits are real, and what are imaginary? How can we leverage our most useful and abundant resource – ourselves? Is it possible to operate a better, free society without trade and government entirely?

The answer is, *yes, of course it is possible*. And in many ways, as I will show you, we already are.

The methods and ideas for an Open Economy beyond

trade and government are already familiar to you. We just need to apply them in new ways.

But an Open Economy is not just about adapting to a new set of parameters in order to survive, it's about embracing a historic opportunity to transcend our primitive, feudalistic methods and create an amazing living paradise for everyone.

Pause for Thought

Before we go any further, I wish to face down those people who will tell you that '*xxx* is not possible', or that 'people are too *xyz* for that to happen'.

This is utter nonsense. We can do *exactly* what we want. We are not hapless passengers strapped into some fixed destiny. We are highly adaptable creatures – as evidenced by our already remarkable evolutionary success. But almost all of our current expectations of life today are based on a *learned, predatory culture*.

We enter the world as blank canvases, so we can program ourselves in any number of ways.

Take a minute to ponder the diversity and breadth of human behaviour across the world, honed by local culture. Consider the remote Patagonian shepherd; the faithful Nepalese sherpa; the resourceful Zulu tribeswoman; the American porn star; the brutal Nazi generals or Islamic fundamentalists; the billionaire playboy; the street beggar; the silent celibate monk; the single mother of four; the prodigious teenage entrepreneur; the hopeless drunk.

Once you detach yourself from judging some as good and some as bad, you can begin to appreciate that these are all *vastly different expressions of the same creature* –

and this is really good news! It shows us just how impressionable we are – depending on our immediate environment and value system.

Look how easily Western society is shaped by pop culture, the latest movies, pop stars, fashion trends, the latest must-have gadget, the hottest Silicon Valley start-up. Look how enraged we become with celebrity scandals that have absolutely no bearing on our lives.

Like it or not, we human beings are extremely malleable and impressionable creatures. But it's good news because it shows we are adaptable. We just need to program ourselves with the 'right stuff'.

The only thing anyone can say with any certainty about 'human nature' is that we are all pre-programmed to do one thing: *survive*. Everything else related to how we behave stems from this program. The desire to succeed, to live in abundance, to be popular, to procreate – they are all merely extensions of our personal desire to survive.

So, when someone says 'people are selfish', what they are actually referring to is the *environment* that teaches and rewards that selfish behaviour.

In short, when it comes down to what is possible in human society, *we can create any type of society we want*. As long as that society is serving people's base desire to survive, then it will flourish.

What is an Open Economy?

I derive the term 'Open Economy' as follows:

> **OPEN:** From the open source software industry: *decentralised, shared, free.* From the general dictionary definition: *unrestricted, honest, transparent.*

> **ECONOMY:** From the original French word *'économie'*, meaning *management of material resources*, and the latinised Greek *'oikonomia'*, meaning *household management*.[3]

So I would define it thus:

An Open Economy is the application of an open, distributed model to the traditionally closed-loop economic system. In other words, rather than every individual seeking only to benefit themselves, a common understanding exists that enables everyone to benefit everyone, including themselves.[4]

---

3   In modern language, the true meaning of the word 'economy' has been lost to wildly convoluted theories and, in my opinion, a particularly dangerous brand of pseudoscience. Economy is a simple concept: *how to distribute resources efficiently and equitably.* As I often say, to define 'economy', just think children and apples – anything more complicated is something else *masquerading* as economics.

4   A little disambiguation is necessary here. In traditional economics, the term 'open economy' is used to refer to the practice of international trading from within a country. This is *not* the definition I am referring to here.

Of course, an Open Economy is not really *just* an economy. It's a whole systems approach to running an optimum, compassionate human society that serves everyone equally. This can only be done by stepping out of our traditional constraints of trade and governance and agreeing on a common purpose.

Everyone wants to live in a better world – there's no doubt about that. But, because we are all trying hard to make a good life for ourselves, the industry and disconnection this creates is actually making things worse for everyone – including ourselves.

An Open Economy is about jointly changing our priorities towards a common purpose. It's about understanding that self-based thinking is no longer serving our long term interest. If we each agree to shift our priorities from 'I' to 'all', we will *all* be better off.

Imagine, for example, a fish barrel and seven people fishing from that barrel. Everyone is trying to catch the most fish to feed themselves. Everyone fishes at more or less the same pace, with no-one able to stop to consider how best to manage the fish supply or maintain water quality, because by doing so, they will lose out on fish themselves. Eventually, through lack of management, the fish will be gone.

Or, the other potential outcome is, one or more people will develop a better tool or technique for catching fish. Pretty soon, they will have all the fish, leaving the others either hungry or subservient to them in some way, e.g. buying their fish.

It's clear from this example that teamwork would be a far better approach. By agreeing to work together and dedicating people to certain tasks like managing supply, preparing and cooking the fish or creating new technology, the group ensures that stocks are managed well and that the best and most sustainable techniques are employed to benefit everyone.

In other words, the people *change their purpose from self-interest to group interest*. This is what successful companies do, they employ teamwork united in a common core goal: higher profits for the company. Being united in that goal creates efficiency.

We are now seven billion people around a fish barrel Earth. There is *no* common goal, and *no* coordinated team effort to manage our society and biosphere in a fair and sustainable way. Trade, governance and division are preventing this from happening.

In an Open Economy, we transcend these limitations, and redress our individual actions and priorities such that we each understand and unite under this common purpose: to create a better life for everyone, and in doing so, create a better life for ourselves.

Our Priorities

The way I see it, we each inhabit three 'domains':

- **My Self** (including immediate family)
- **My Community** (neighbours, peers, colleagues)
- **My World** (everything else)

We prioritise them in that order, which is quite normal. What is wrong, however, is how we space those priorities. If we drew this again on a ladder of, say, ten steps, it might look something like this:

1. **My Self**
2.
3.
4.
5. **My Community**
6.
7.
8.
9.
10. **My World**

Look familiar? Maybe you would place things slightly differently, but you get the idea. If it's still not obvious, then consider the following (this might sting a bit):

1. **My Self**
2. My Property
3. My Religion / Spiritual Beliefs
4. My Status / Public Perception
5. **My Community**
6. My Favourite Sport Team
7. My Job / Company
8. My Country
9. My Favourite TV Show
10. **My World**

Obviously, this is merely to demonstrate a point and not to be taken literally, but the point is clear: *our priorities for life's non-essentials are too high, and for life's essentials too low.* Whatever we believe about sports or religion, we literally *can't survive* without our community and our world, yet we don't attribute the corresponding importance to them.

We need to ascribe the same religious importance that we do to our country, family or spiritual beliefs - to our *entire living community and shared planetary home.*

That's not a hippie ideal. It's not some delusional utopia. It's not communism. It's just *physics.*

We are all inextricably linked to each other and our living planetary home. Competition inside a closed system is self-destruction.

Obviously, when it comes to priorities, we can't put anything more important than ourselves – that doesn't make any sense. But we need to get closer to:

1. **My Self**

2. **My Community**

3. **My World**

4. ...everything else

5. ...everything else

Each of these three domains is essential to our lives. We need to have utmost respect for each, and to understand them and their interconnection as fundamental to our being.

Shifting Our Priorities

So how do we change our priorities? In two ways.

The first is the same way we skewed them – through mass media information campaigns and advertising. We have all the tools in place to do it: TV, radio, print media and the internet.

Just as we have been taught consumerism, insecurity and envy through the repetitious advertising of products, so we can also disseminate a revised value system, demonstrating the practical benefits of working towards this common purpose of taking care of each other and planet.

A good example in which we have already made huge advances in shaping our behaviour is recycling – through widespread media initiatives. In less than twenty years almost everyone in Western society has changed their dumping habits and embraced recycling, thanks to those media campaigns.

There's no doubt that once a new way of thinking becomes fashionable, it spreads like wildfire. Media has shown us this time and time again. So let's start by admitting just how impressionable and socially motivated we are, then use it to our advantage.

If we can be programmed to worship icons, obey other

people, buy toxic stuff, and be distracted by irrelevant news, then we can easily be programmed to care about what matters and act towards the greater good.

In short, we need to start re-programming ourselves with the 'right stuff'.

The second way of shifting our priorities is in our daily actions. Since we are social, our habits are highly infectious. Those of us who are already aware of where our priorities need to be can 'be the change' by altering our habits to reflect the new way of thinking. Many people are already doing so and it's spreading fast.

Recycling was just the beginning. It doesn't stop there. We need to shift our habits to be more inclusive, to engage more with our communities, to re-connect with nature, to share freely what we can and offer help to each other unconditionally.

Sharing is perhaps the most powerful and clear demonstration of intent. But let's be clear. By sharing, I don't mean everyone in the world holding hands and singing *kum-ba-yah*. That's probably never going to happen. I mean sharing where interpersonal and community cooperation become *second nature* and *basic human courtesies*, just like politeness and manners are today.

Imagine how quickly our world will change when unconditional sharing becomes epidemic?

Removing Our Artificial Limits

Anything that divides or constrains people and does not exist in the physical realm is an artificial social construct. Such divisions between people that restrict normal moral behaviour create inefficiency, inequality and animosity. For example:

- Borders – restricting free movement of people
- Money / trade – limiting access to resources
- Social class – wealth inequality
- Exclusive ownership – reducing access to potentially shareable resources
- States / laws – constraining rights through citizenship
- Intellectual property – reducing the ability to improve others' work
- Religion / Race – cultural or tribal animosity[5]

As we begin to shift our priorities to what matters, the artificial social constructs that divide people will start to become more obvious – and more obviously unnecessary to people.

---

5   Struggle between race and religion can almost always be traced back to class or resource struggle of some kind rather than culture.

These divisions, like laws, only exist because of lack of understanding and empathy.

Since they exist only in our collective imagination, the only way to remove them is to 'un-imagine' them. This is done by simply *exposing* them in stark relief to the things that *do* matter. As we collectively shift our focus to the real stuff, we will naturally let go of the imaginary. We always prioritise what we focus on.

History is full of incidences of 'fact' quickly becoming fable as new thinking arrives. Remember when smoking tobacco was good for you? Or when black people and women were seen as inferior beings? Or when the Sun revolved around the Earth?

Our ideas and conceptions are continually developing. Some day all our nations will become mere geographical regions. Social class, poverty and inequality will become curios of history. Money and enforced labour – unimaginable.

And when we dissolve these imaginary divisions, we are automatically forced to become more connected, and our understanding of each other grows.

Understanding is the key to empathy, compassion – and ultimately peace.

Living in an Open Economy

Most people who have given any consideration to a moneyless society are already aware that we have the technology to create a world of abundance, without the constraints and inequality of trade and governance, owing to how much human labour can now be efficiently automated.

Without scarcity, and a massive reduction in the need for labour, money effectively becomes obsolete. That's the theory. But it's not the full story, nor does it convince most people who come into contact with the theory.

In my opinion, this kind of super-advanced 'Star Trek' moneyless society is still quite a distance away – not because we lack the technology – but because we lack the understanding required to make it work.

A truly free society should be just that – unlimited, self-determining and self-organising for the optimum benefit of all. We don't actually need technology to achieve this, we just need to collectively alter our priorities. So what about the general day-to-day business of an Open Economy? How would society work? How do we maintain a degree of order and efficiency in a totally free society without coercion?

Social Gravity

First things first: Social Gravity – this is the basic glue that keeps society together. We are a social species. By and large, we prefer to do things together. Hence we gravitate into groups, teams, villages and cities.

This all stems from one basic human need – the urge to belong. Everything from our cities, our cultures, our religions, even our great unwritten social contract of be-good-to-others – stems from this need.

Social Gravity is the force that naturally binds us – even keeping our unfair, outdated system together, with all its flaws. This is because most people prefer to accept the broader consensus rather than apply radical new thinking. The fact that it keeps our system together, in plain view of its injustices and suffering, tells you just how powerful a force Social Gravity is.

Now imagine how much *more* powerful this force could be in a society that positively promotes life, health, diversity and happiness for all. Social Gravity is the *primary force* that will bond an Open Economy and make it work.

Currently, most Open Economy advocates are fighting against Social Gravity as they meet peoples' resistance to break from familiar ideas and norms. But we know this is changing more by the day as these people are beginning to question the logic and injustice of the prevailing system themselves.

As more people change their viewpoint, the more they 'normalise' the environment for others to do so too. This is why it's important to let people know about this new way of thinking. Even if they disagree now, you may become a point of reference for them later.

Social Gravity is what will maintain order, balance and efficiency in an Open Economy. The more people benefit from it, the stronger that force becomes.

Self–Determination

Most people do not understand the true meaning of anarchy – to the point that I've almost given up using the term. Over the years, the media and prevailing thought have confused its meaning with disorder, chaos and violence. But this is not anarchy – this is usually just the collapse of oppression.

Our screens are often filled with views of young people rioting, throwing missiles or looting shops, with the strong suggestion that they have become 'lawless', or that 'law and order' need to be restored. This is a very serious misunderstanding.

Scenes like this are, in fact, the *backlash of oppression*. Whatever happened *before* is what created those scenes. This is *anger*, not anarchy. This is very important to remember.[6]

The best way to describe anarchy is to look to the animal kingdom. By and large, animals are peaceful creatures and will happily co-exist with each other in a steady-state[7] environment. The only time an animal is

---

6   One could easily be forgiven for thinking that this 'misunderstanding' is deliberately perpetuated by the media. ;)

7   A steady state environment is an environment where scarcity and territories are not an issue. In an Open Economy, regaining community trust and achieving abundance would bring about this steady-state environment.

ever violent is when it must kill to eat, or when threatened.

This is self-determination – the *default behaviour of all beings*. When survival is not threatened, peaceful coexistence is the default state of all animals, including humans. It's simply easier than violence.

History books and media are full of references to aggressive culture, heinous acts of violence and torture – man pitted against fellow man. This gives an abiding impression of a bloodthirsty homo sapiens, indiscriminately bludgeoning all in his path to get what he wants. But this is a *false* impression, and yet another dangerous misunderstanding of the world and of ourselves.

The reason for this is simple. Wars, conflict and aggression make for more interesting stories so are always reported on and read about in our history books and media. Whereas, peace and non-conflict is essentially boring and does not get written about – yet it probably accounts for 99.999% of all human behaviour.

For every lunatic who takes up a gun and starts shooting people, there are millions and millions of other people who *don't*, but we never hear about them. The reality is, our human experience, from a statistical point of view, is almost entirely peaceful.

A self-determining society doesn't use or require laws.

Laws were invented primarily to protect private interests and enforce the payment of taxes. In a world of abundance, greater connection and understanding of ourselves, these laws would become redundant.

We are a social species. We *want* to get along. We all experience this spirit of humanity every day in the help we get from our work or student colleagues, our friends and families, and from strangers – even in times of crisis. When external stresses are gone, people are good to each other.

As long as we each have our survival needs met by society, there is nothing to compete for – at least nothing that is worth killing or dying for.

Of course, we cannot expect self-determination to rule out all acts of senseless violence or anti-social behaviour, but once scarcity is not an object to people's existence, we can certainly expect to reduce such incidences to a minimum. (See *Anti-Aggression Strategies, p.57*)

It's worth pointing out that senseless violence and anti-social behaviour are *already common daily occurrences* under our current law system – almost all of which can be related directly to scarcity and inequality. It's frankly absurd to suggest such behaviour would increase in an abundant, compassionate society.

Natural Boundaries

Have you ever had a guest staying at your house, in one of your rooms? It's your house, and you can go where you like, but, when someone is staying with you – even if they aren't in the room – you feel like that room is 'theirs'? Like you can't just walk in and get something from that room without asking them first?

This feeling of not-being-where-you're-supposed-to-be is our already built-in sense of personal boundary. You feel like you are encroaching on someone else's space.

It is a natural sense of respect for the privacy and boundaries of others. This is where our modern notion of ownership comes from – not the other way around. Ownership is an attempt to formalise and quantify this inner sense. Of course, we know just how much this exclusive ownership mechanism has caused problems with monopolisation of resources, concentration of wealth, and marginalisation of those who can't pay the asking price.

Losing the ability to concentrate wealth or hog resources in an Open Economy will have no effect on our natural and implied property rights. The home you own today would be just as much your home in an Open Economy through our natural sense of personal boundaries and respect for privacy.

Open Education

To give an Open Economy any chance of succeeding or surviving, a radical overhaul of our current education system is essential. By and large, our current system prioritises reading, writing and arithmetic as core learning, but these are far from the most important skills we need to acquire.

Children from the earliest age *must* have access to the most important information that can help them live a rich and fulfilling life, with all the skills for building great self, interpersonal and community relationships. This information can easily be compiled for children of all levels of cognisance.

The best way to approach education, I think, is to begin with the three domains that I mentioned earlier: *Self, Community* and *World*. In each of these three domains can be taught three levels of insight: *Awareness, Respect* and *Understanding*.

Awareness of Self, Community and World being the most basic, leading to Respect, then on to Understanding, where the daily practicalities of each are learned. Here are some examples of topic headings which could be extrapolated from these core insights:

Awareness

➢ **Self:** *realisation of self, basic body functions, life, breathing, the senses, self-awareness, meditation.*

➢ **Community:** *position in the community, affirming equality, trust, compassion and empathy.*

➢ **World:** *place within the world, the cycle of life, other species, the balance of nature, the food chain.*

Respect

➢ **Self:** *self-love, respect and responsibility.*

➢ **Community:** *the purpose of kinship and empathy.*

➢ **World:** *the fragility of life systems, resources.*

Understanding

➢ **Self:** *basic anatomy, hygiene, nutrition, hydration, coping with negative feelings, problem solving, food preparation, creativity, realising full potential.*

➢ **Community:** *the purpose of sharing, community service, leadership, teamwork, interpersonal relationships, effective communication, sex, parenting and family, responsibility, resolving disputes.*

➢ **World:** *water and food systems, agricultural techniques, energy production, efficiency, economy, technology, improving natural habitat.*

Also, our current education model has conformity and fact-repetition built in, which does nothing to inspire creativity or individuality in students. This is mainly because of the single teacher and standardised test model. The teacher in this environment is usually under pressure to achieve specific results and becomes nothing more than a dictator of facts.

In an Open Education system, we can employ group learning techniques – mixing students together to fact-find and discover for themselves as a group. This way, learning becomes a multi-directional and social experience, with the teacher merely acting as navigator to help students get to the information they want.

Also, in group learning – and without standardised testing – there is no necessity to separate students strictly according to age. Students of every age have something to learn, whether through discovery, instruction, or even by teaching other students themselves.

Multi-age classes would also do away with the unrealistic competition between children of similar age and development, while also reflecting a far more accurate analogy of the real world.

Standardised academic tests would give way to periodical aptitude tests, to help orientate students towards their optimum talents.

The primary purpose of learning should be to create

adults who can reach the summit of their unique potential, with a keen understanding of – and respect for – the world, community and *person* they are in.

Without a dog-eat-dog society, education can be more fun, engaging, relaxed and self-organising, affording children the opportunity to carve their own path without fear of failure.

Of course language, arithmetic and general facts will still be taught in an Open Education system, but the relevant, practical lessons on life, respect and social skills *must take precedence* in order to create better, happier people.

Note: There is no reason why elements of the Open Education system could not be introduced today.

Community Service

While many necessary jobs in the community will naturally be filled by those passionate enough to devote their time unconditionally to it – e.g. teachers, doctors and skilled trades, etc. – there will invariably be a shortfall in volunteers to participate in some of the less glamorous functions of modern society – like sweeping the roads, clearing drains, painting public buildings, etc.

Community service is a concept that most of us are already familiar with – though we usually associate it with punishment for petty criminals. But the fact is, organised community service is undoubtedly the most efficient way to deliver essential services equitably within a large population.

Just because a society is not based on coercion, doesn't mean it can't be highly organised. In the enactment of an Open Economy, every member of the community would be asked to contribute a reasonable minimum number of hours per month to dedicate to their community and the greater good. This would be a core component in everyone's Life Education.

Also, remember that for a society without conventional employment, those community service hours would be a trivial commitment for most people.

A monthly schedule of required services and tasks in the community could be published, where members would opt in to participate in whichever tasks best suited their skills and availability at the time.

The number of recommended hours per month would obviously depend on local factors, i.e. what needed to be done, population number, availability of skills, complexity of tasks, etc., but the idea is to keep people's commitment to a minimum by spreading the community workload as widely as possible.

Children should also be actively encouraged to engage in their community's projects from as young as possible – and in as many diverse tasks as possible. This would help them discover their own aptitude, engage with the community, and gain valuable life experience in the process.

There's no reason why community work in a free world should ever be onerous or could not be carried out in entertaining ways. For example, with a little imagination, some tasks could even be turned into sports events where teams compete to fulfil tasks or see who can come up with the most innovative solutions.

The overriding goal is that community service, while providing essential services, would also be a fulfilling and engaging experience that people would enjoy.

Resource Allocation

An Open Economy does not need money or governance in order to be organised. It just needs common purpose and an effective information network to maintain its efficiency. Every community would have its own central information hub – a complete inventory of resources, people and skills in the area. Such a database would be maintained and moderated by users and connected to every other community worldwide.

The resources section would be a map-based inventory and requisition facility for users to list, find and request the resources they require. By resources, I mean anything from raw iron ore to a wooden dining table. Whatever physical resources people have available for sharing, they can list it on the database.

Anyone looking for those resources would simply run a search on the database, find the nearest match, and place a requisition order. If necessary, resource requisitions could be weighted according to urgency and depth of benefit to the community.

For example, a community urgently requiring concrete for reconstruction of a well would have greater priority than an individual requiring concrete to build a garage.

Like the inventory, the requisition system would be entirely transparent, and a user making the request would be able to see where his request was positioned in the queue and read the other requests. A fully transparent system is the only way to avoid needless misunderstandings and conflicts.

Items that need to be delivered from one area to another could then come under the Community Service system in the dispatching area to source a driver and truck to carry the requested goods – if possible on an already existing dispatch route.

The skills section would be a map-based directory of people who wish to offer their labour or specialist skills to others. Users looking for those skills would be able to make contact with them directly.

Every community, like today, would have its own 'store' or depot where people go to get the things that they need like food, clothes, etc. Store stocks would be managed by people merely inputting what they are taking, or what they need in the future. The supply and demand is simply the rolling record of user data, always updating and optimizing itself.

Anyone who produces food and goods in the area could also stock the store themselves with whatever excess produce they have. Likewise, people in the community would take turns to manage or clean the store, etc.

Organic Leadership

Just because a self-determining society doesn't use governance doesn't mean that we don't need leaders and role models. Leaders are people who see further, can envision greater possibilities, can solve problems, or have the extra courage and enthusiasm to inspire people during uncertain times. In an Open Economy people will still seek leaders to inspire and help them.

This does not mean that we need rulers. Rulers do not necessarily help or inspire, they merely rule – usually without qualification – making occasional diktats.

However, some kind of leadership structure is undoubtedly an efficient way of accomplishing complex tasks. (Think film director, for instance.) In Organic Leadership, team leaders would be nominated for specific tasks by the team itself, based on their ability, and for the life of that task.

A true leader's role is merely to administrate the desires of others or to adjudicate on which suggested course of action is the best one. Leadership in this form will only exist as and for when it is necessary and based on the common understanding that once chosen, the leader has final say on matters for which they are appointed.

A Project Pledge Scheme

In any community, large projects will always need to be undertaken – like building a new bridge, road, school or hospital. The current market system works quite well in this regard, as it monetarily 'locks in' the required personnel to complete large scale tasks uninterrupted for many months or years at a time.

In a moneyless world, rotating volunteer personnel from within local communities to help with long, complex projects may prove inefficient or, in some cases, unworkable.

A solution would be to create a Project Pledge Scheme, where willing workers publicly pledge to see the project through until completion.

It's reasonable to assume that any large-scale community project would find it easy to enlist local volunteers who would benefit directly from the project, but a greater level of commitment to any large project is required.

Each participant could attend a project launch ceremony where they each undertake their pledges. What's important is that the project managers would seek the full commitment and pledge from the participants at the *outset*, so that the volunteers themselves become personally and emotionally invested in the project's success too. Most people, when working in teams, don't want to be the one to 'let the side down'.

As with all community service, large projects would also have a strong emphasis on creating an enjoyable social experience for the participants.

As technology gets better and becomes more widely available, large intensive projects would obviously require fewer and fewer human personnel, but a Project Pledge Scheme could be a viable interim solution.

A Community Awards System

Obviously, the notion of giving for reward is firmly embedded in our culture. It's not entirely clear to me if we can ever fully transcend this essentially ego-based reward paradigm – or even if transcending this would be a good idea.

Many supporters of an Open Economy believe we can surpass ego. I'm not so sure, since at its most base level, ego is part of our survival mechanism, and, in its highest form, embodies our individuality. Certainly in the interim period, moving from a market-based system to an Open Economy, I believe it will be useful to maintain some symbolic reward or honour system.

A Community Awards System[8] would be a symbolic payment method – a utility that provides the means to award and demonstrate your appreciation for any person you wish, thereby aggregating their public reputation score.

The awards would have no usable value and are simply tokens of esteem. In a world powered purely by volunteerism, appreciation will be a valuable incentive.

---

8   A good example already exists today. HonorPay (honorpay.org) has many users, providing people with a means of incentive and reward beyond physical or monetary tokens.

An Open Proposals Platform

In matters relating to large numbers of people, it would make sense to have an open platform where each person can vote on decisions that affect everybody, voice their opinions, and propose motions of their own.

In an online community hub, this would be simple to implement and would seem to be a basic prerequisite for an open society.

Any member could propose any idea for improving their community, then other members would vote up or down and comment on the proposal. This would be an invaluable way to steer the community.

Surprisingly, it may end up seeing little use, since a more conscious, abundant society will likely have moved beyond reducing everything to binary choices and leaving an endless trail of disgruntled minorities!

However, there may be another far more interesting and useful purpose for such a technology if implemented today.

Today, even in supposedly democratic countries, most important decisions relating to things like budgets, laws, jobs or foreign conflict are never put to a public referendum.

Implementing a public polling platform today would give people the opportunity to 'vote' on every issue that affects their lives. Even if that vote did not 'officially' count, it would still give them a means for their collective voice to be heard. For instance, it would be much more difficult for a country's government to follow through on its policy when an open voting platform has clearly shown a large majority of the population don't agree with it.

Such a platform could play a very important role in bringing about change, while also bringing the required technology for post-change society.

Creative Arbitration

No matter how well we design or create the kind of world we want to see, there will always be disputes among people, whether over relationships, personal beliefs, or claims on land or property. That is just part of the deal with being human. We aren't perfect – so it's best to begin by accepting that fact!

By far the most crucial instrument in resolving disputes is speed. Unresolved problems create stress, animosity and compound fear. These are the explosive ingredients of aggression and war, so the sooner a solution is found, the better.

Where people are unable to find solutions themselves, it would seem reasonable for both parties to nominate an independent arbitrator whom they both trust to help them reach a solution. (The arbitrator could be anyone from the community who is willing to help.)

But let's define what we mean by 'solution'. In today's world, resolutions are usually reached using the law or courts to decide. It almost always comes down to a binary choice where one side wins and the other loses. There's nothing wrong with this in theory, but to create a lasting, stable society, *no-one* should ever need to be the loser.

For example, if two parties *A* and *B* are arguing over property rights, and an arbitrator – acting in the interest of the community – decides that *A* is the more deserving claimant, it may please *A* and the community, but still leaves *B* the loser. Even though *B* may accept that resolution, they are left with a sense of personal injustice and/or embarrassment that can ferment into one of the previously mentioned ingredients of aggression. This is unnecessary.

I propose that each party should first be asked to detail their complaint and preferred outcome to the other, then encouraged to offer a range of solutions that fulfils theirs and the other's requirements – regardless of impossibility. This mental exercise invokes empathy, thereby creating a pathway to a workable, mutually beneficial solution.

In an Open Economy, we should *never* settle for a resolution that leaves even one person marginalised. This is a limited view. There is *always* a creative solution that brings an optimal – and preferably superior – outcome for everyone, and nothing should be considered solved until such a solution is found.

Once the limits of traditional society are lifted, much more solutions become available. For example, why would someone want to claim your house if they could readily organise an even better one for themselves elsewhere?

Creative Arbitration is about finding that amazing solution that makes all parties happier than before. We shouldn't settle for less. The best persons to assist in dispute resolution ought not necessarily to be those wisest, but those most flexible and creative in problem-solving.

Anti–Aggression Strategies

Implementing a free and abundant Open Economy is undoubtedly the best way to reduce the incidences and causes of socially aberrant behaviour, but of course, we are not perfect and some violence and anti-social behaviour will still arise – albeit many times less than before.

Having a system of prescribed laws and measures to tackle 'crime' will neither be possible nor desirable in a self-determining society, so what is the solution? How do we stop people perpetrating violence on others? How do we stop people who take unfair advantage? How do we punish people? Should we punish people at all?

The answer is simple: apply common sense.

Every situation is unique and should be handled according to that situation, using local information, with respect to the people involved, and the application of common sense. Creative Arbitration can be applied to resolve disputes and find an optimal outcome if appropriate, but if it's not possible and someone is continually making life difficult for others or is being violent, then they need to be restrained. It's that simple.

For example, common sense dictates that you don't allow a gunman to continue his killing spree uninterrupted. He will obviously be restrained. How and in what measure would be determined by the situation. Drastic force may be required.

In the event that someone does have to be restrained, it would be crucial to re-integrate that individual back into the wider community as soon as possible, as that is their best hope of re-evaluating their actions or behaviour. People who feel valued and appreciated by others rarely have use for aggression.

In today's world, a prison is merely a place to lock people up out of harm's way, but there are plenty of effective rehabilitation strategies and techniques available today that can be employed and improved on, which may be too expensive or labour intensive to be successfully implemented.

An Open Economy would have no such restrictions – and presumably much fewer detainees – with plenty of good counsellors on hand, passionate enough about their work to put in the time.

But restraint is still restraint, and would obviously be the absolute last resort of an Open Economy, but it's pointless to pretend that drastic action would not be taken in drastic circumstances where common sense is employed.

A Community Lighthouse

In order to prevent social decay or regression back to our former feudal ways, an Open Economy would require some early warning protection system. This could perhaps be incorporated into the Open Proposals platform and act like an immune system for the community at large.

If there are problems in some areas with resources or people, where the quality of life is becoming less than optimal, then members of that community should be able to raise alerts – anonymously if desired – to warn the greater community of the problem.

As previously stated, speed is the key to finding effective solutions and applying a creative problem-solving approach.

For example, say a remote village is being denied some vital resource due to the actions of a local farmer. A problem like this, if ignored, could end in some violent confrontation, which, in turn, could lead to repercussions and a larger tribal conflict, etc.

A Community Lighthouse system could alert a neighbouring community who may be able to intervene quickly, impartially and creatively arbitrate a solution, or, failing that, find an alternative means of providing that resource to the community. It may even suffice for that farmer himself to be alerted as to how unpopular he is becoming.

All major conflicts spring from unresolved small problems. By resolving small problems early and efficiently, we can avoid the larger ones completely. A Community Lighthouse system would seem to be a prerequisite to the ongoing stability of an Open Economy.

'Real Life' Stories

One of the most effective ways of conveying new ideas like an Open Economy is in the form of fictional accounts of people in various scenarios, and how the Open Economy might impact and improve their lives.[9]

Here are a few examples to help you visualise it:

Geoff the Postal Worker

As a postman, Geoff was no stranger to early morning starts. He arrived at the postal depot every weekday morning at 6.30am to begin his round and finished every day around 3pm. He was doing well for money and very happy with his basement apartment.

When the Open Economy came, Geoff, like most people was a little confused but excited at the prospect of not having to get up so early every day and do the same thing. Shortly after the announcement, Geoff was called to the depot for a staff meeting. His boss Julio was in a surprisingly good mood.

"As some of you have probably heard," Julio said, "the OE Transition Panel have been sending out guidelines to all major service companies over the last few

---

[9] My novel *F-Day: The Second Dawn Of Man* is a full-length dramatisation of events leading to a global Open Economy which you might also find interesting.

months..."

Geoff didn't know but was intrigued. Julio went on.

"Basically the guidelines are as follows: working here at the postal service is now optional for all staff. This is no longer a profit enterprise and subsequently, there will be no more wages. So any work undertaken here is now purely voluntary..."

There were some stifled laughs from the workers.

"But," Julio continued, "the better news is that now there's going to be a lot less post to deliver. Pretty much eighty percent of post these days is made up of invoices, reminders and account statements. Obviously, all that is gone, but there will still be some items that people want to send to each other."

"So, for anyone who is still interested in working here on a voluntary basis, we will need about twenty percent of the same man-hours that you were doing before. That means around eight hours per week. You can split that into two four-hour days or whatever way you like. Or, you can do less by rotating your hours with one or more others."

That sounded reasonable to Geoff. Maybe he could arrange with one of the other guys to do two eight-hour days one week, then a full week off the next.

"Oh yes... also," Julio cut in laughing, "we don't need those crazy early morning starts either..."

Everyone chuckled.

"Business, as usual, is over!" Julio proclaimed. "The depot will open at 9am from now on..."

There were spontaneous cheers.

"The only thing we need," Julio continued, "is that you give a firm commitment to the hours you would like to do – and to honour that commitment. We need that to be able to give an efficient service."

"OK, anyone who wants to sign up and pledge their hours, can they please come forward and I'll start taking names? Thanks."

Geoff stood his ground to see what would happen. To his surprise, many people moved forward, and many, like him, were also looking around to see what others would do. Geoff moved forward and pledged his sixteen hours a week. Julio thanked him and handed him the form.

Looking back, Geoff noticed around three or four of the workers leaving the building having made no pledge, but the other forty or so stayed, chatted and made their pledges too.

He overheard one of the guys asking Julio what would happen if he changed his mind.

"No problem at all, James," Julio said, "but just give us enough notice so we can reorganise the roster, OK?"

Bill, Jenny, Jackie and Tyson

Bill had been unemployed for almost three years after the local metal fabricators closed. Thankfully, Jenny had managed to keep her job at the movie theatre, but they'd been struggling. Thirteen year old Jackie's high-school books - never mind her newfound interest in boys and fashion! - had been bleeding them dry. Eight year old Tyson was a great kid who never complained, even though they had been shocked to hear about him being bullied at school.

In their town, the Open Economy had kind of crept in, as so much unemployment had forced people into seeking sharing alternatives. So, when the local government made the announcement, it was less of a shock and more of a relief. Now that it was 'official' they could finally organise themselves.

Immediately, Jenny left the movie house forever and headed to the school to offer herself as a teacher. She had read the new Life Education Manual that had been passed around the schools over the last year and was supremely impressed. Finally, an education that focused on creating better people – not workers – and didn't leave anyone behind. She was ready to sign up, so other kids would never have to endure what Tyson had endured.

Bill had tears in his eyes the day the metal factory re-opened. All the machinery was still there intact and gathering dust. Obviously, even the liquidators thought it was too much trouble to remove them. The old owner of the factory had re-opened it for the community and to help with the new greenhouse constructions that had been suggested by the OE Planning Committee. Bill had put his name down straight away.

Jackie was amazed when her Mum sat her down and asked her if she would like to become a teacher in the school.

"Mom, I'm only thirteen," she protested.

"It doesn't matter sweetie," Jenny said. "Things don't work like that anymore. We are all learning, and we are all teachers. By helping the younger kids, you're learning too. It's called group learning."

"So I get to teach Tyson?" she teased, giving him a mock evil grin.

"Yes!" Tyson shouted, jumping up off the seat.

"No," Jenny insisted. "You both get to teach each other."

Margaret

Since her husband died twenty years ago, Margaret had never ceased surprising herself. The small vineyard they had bought together – which Charles had almost run into the ground – was now a multi-million Euro enterprise, thanks to her hitherto unknown business acumen.

After many tough years and sharp decisions, she had single-handedly turned the place into a little goldmine, employing more than thirty staff.

When she heard about the plans for an Open Economy from her neighbour, she was furious. After all her hard work building up an empire, it was all just going to be worthless? She would fight it tooth and nail when it came to a vote.

One day a large packet came, addressed from the local OE Planning Team. She swore and threw it aside.

Later her daughter came home, rescued the packet from the trash and began to look through it.

"Mom," she said, "you know you really ought to read this. This looks, er, amazing..."

"Oh no, not you too dear," Margaret groaned. "It's like Invasion of the Body-Snatchers around this town now."

Later that evening, after Millie had gone home, Margaret picked up the brochure that her daughter had clearly left strategically opened on the coffee table. *'How The Open Economy Will Affect Your Business'* was the matter-of-fact title. She started reading:

'Why are you in business?

'Most likely for two reasons: to make something useful, and to make money.

'In an Open Economy, we don't use money. It's about creating a compassionate society where we value community to the extent that we provide for each other without precondition. If we all engage in this, we can realise amazing abundance for everyone – and not just a select few.

'So, if you started out in business purely to make money, then the Open Economy is about to save you all that effort, so you can enjoy a life of abundance without all the stress of running a business.

'If, however, you started out in business to make something useful, then please continue doing so! While continuing to play an important role in your community, you now have the possibility of making that 'something' to the very best of your potential...'

Margaret was perplexed. "How do I make better wine with no staff and no suppliers?" she muttered. She read on.

'Imagine if all your employees were engaged – not for the money you pay them – but for the love of what they make

— just like you?

'In an Open Economy, everyone works at what they love, and the jobs left over are rotated among the community. When you announce to your staff that we are introducing an Open Economy and everyone is now a volunteer, you know the ones who stay with you are the ones as passionate as you...'

Margaret tried to envisage that scenario — making the announcement and trying to imagine who would stay. Offhand, she could immediately think of five high-level staff who would definitely stay, and a few others who would probably leave. In fact, come to think of it, the ones she imagined leaving were the ones she would be quite glad to see the back of! And maybe, if the Open Economy did come, the people most passionate about wine-making would come to her looking to help out?

She supposed that if all the pickers left, maybe they could rotate that job among the community? Then she remembered all those summers when the students descended on her, looking for work and free lodgings. They didn't just pick, they had the time of their lives.

She was in two minds about it now. She could see how it was feasible, and — she supposed — they would just find a way to make it work anyway.

And maybe, who knows, working purely for the love of it was the best way to make the loveliest wine?

Shelley and Mark

It was five years to the day when the Open Economy was announced in Mark and Shelley's city. Though it wasn't really their city anymore, as they had moved around many times since. Now in their early thirties, they had just arrived back for the fifth-anniversary celebrations.

In the last five years, they had lived in seventeen countries, finding houses on the 'hub and dipping into local communities. Everywhere they had stayed they lived well, worked on some fantastic projects and made great friends. From the great solar arrays in Spain, the high-rise autofarm project outside Moscow, the Baltic cruise ships, the Greenland glacier-banking project, to the Mexican soy and spelt farms, even flying a plane in the Brazilian seed-bombing initiative.

They were really passionate about their planet. Like many others, they had watched the movies that had come out in Year Two from the Open Humanity Group, with their inspiring *Clean Earth* education campaign.

Now they were finally home to see how their city had changed, and, when they emerged from the train station, the change was obvious. The air was clear and clean. No ticket barriers. No security staff. The street was quiet except for a distant dog barking.

Yet, cars were passing.

"Ah," Mark said. "Electric cars! So quiet."

Looking up and down the street, they saw lots of people on bicycles, walking dogs, chatting and playing in what looked like a new adult play area.

"Can't you see it?" Shelley asked Mark suddenly.

"Er, see what?" Mark replied.

"There's no-one rushing around…"

"Ahh, you're right," Mark exclaimed, "and," he said, looking around again, "there's no-one wearing suits!"

"Ha ha!!" Shelley burst out laughing.

"Do you remember," he said taking her hand, "meeting me in that park over there on your lunch break…"

"Yes, and my heel broke off on the way back to work…" she started giggling. "I remember the way my boss looked at me when I came back to the office in bare feet…ha ha… so stern and so serious…"

"Boss!" Mark exploded. "How ridiculous that sounds!"

Their laughter was suddenly interrupted by a large black shadow that came over them. They looked up.

Above them was a giant silver airship in the shape of a teddy bear, with people waving down at them from the windows. Mark looked at Shelley.

"Looks like the celebrations are starting early," he shouted. "Come on!"

Into The Open Economy

So, how do we get there?

To most people, the idea of a moneyless 'utopia' is certainly desirable – but maybe in a hundred years or so. The only reason they think that is because the idea is so remote to their conventional thinking. Of course, money is absolutely integral to our lives right now, so this is an understandable reaction.

But there are two reasons why this is false. 1) So much of what defines an Open Economy is already happening today, and 2) We typically underestimate the speed of social change once an idea takes hold.

It's Already Happening

The internet and the open source movement have proved beyond doubt that amazing things can happen in a voluntary domain. Great examples are Linux – one of the most popular operating systems in the world, Google Chrome (aka Chromium) is the most popular browser in the world, and Android the most popular mobile device software. These are all developed purely by volunteers all over the world, in a self-organising process called 'forking' where the best ideas and approaches naturally win out.

We have seen the rise of free internet content – Youtube, Wikipedia, Yahoo, Google, Facebook, etc. Although most of these have incorporated advertising into their business model now, they all began – and made their mark – as purely voluntary services. Younger generations today expect to get content like music, videos and software for free because that is now the norm.

A quick search of the internet will also reveal the rise of free-minded projects springing up everywhere. 'Pay as you feel' or 'contributionism' business initiatives, where you pay only what you want; sites where people offer free goods, swaps and services like *Freecycle, Free World Network, Timebanks, Streetbank* are all becoming widely used. Eco building projects like Open Source Ecology and Natural Homes offer easy and better solutions for building a home for next to nothing. A plethora of 'end of capitalism' movements like *Occupy Wall St., Anonymous, The Free World Charter, Ubuntu, The Venus Project, The Zeitgeist Movement*, etc. are all implicating a collaborative and moneyless economy as the only viable future. Many famous and well respected people like Russell Brand, Lee Camp, Paul Mason (journalist) and Jeremy Rifkin (govt. adviser) are using their celebrity to lift the lid on what's really going on, and what new possibilities there are. It's only a matter of time before many more celebrities join them.

Even sites like Uber and AirBnb are showing us how people-powered collaborative enterprise is destroying the old model of centralised control.

But, besides what is happening now, there are many ways an Open Economy has *always* been happening right in front of our eyes.

We are, each of us, members of various exclusive 'clubs'. Our families, our friends, our work colleagues, our neighbours. Time and time again in our lives, we are voluntary contributors to these 'clubs', giving unconditionally, or calling on them when we need assistance ourselves, e.g. your brother needs a lift, a colleague needs help fixing something, you run an errand for a friend, you need to borrow a friend's lawnmower, etc.

To most of us, these acts of unconditional giving and sharing are so automatic that we don't pay them any heed, yet these are the very transactions that make human society function, and are the DNA building blocks of an Open Economy.

And it's not just helping out the people you know and love. We also help out people we don't know. Most of us will rush to help when we see someone who has fallen or dropped something; we give money to charities to help strangers in need; we pull together in times of crisis – even when it may be dangerous to do so; we try our best to help a stranger who asks us for directions; we hold the door open for someone coming behind us.

These are all the enablers of an Open Economy, already happening today – and we are all doing it!

The behaviour and precedent for natural collaboration are already there. We just have to extend it beyond our friends and families, beyond those times of crisis, beyond the necessity of reward, towards a global sense of kinship and mutual responsibility.

The behavioural step required is a small one, and once we see it reciprocated by others, then the behaviour becomes cemented in our psyche. *When we benefit from a behaviour, we tend to repeat that behaviour.*

The Speed Of Social Change

Because we are so connected socially, new information on our 'network' spreads really fast. When someone devises a great new invention or makes an amazing discovery, everyone knows about it really fast.

When mobile phones came out, they were revolutionary. Immediately everyone wanted one. Of course, the technology was still quite primitive and prohibitively expensive, but the demand from people was such that we pushed the technology forward to make it happen very quickly. Within twenty years, almost every person on the planet today has a mobile phone.

But what about behavioural changes? The best example in recent times has got to be recycling. In the early nineties, governments started coming under pressure from environmental scientists about the perils of climate change.

This kind of social change is very different from the mobile phone example because no-one directly benefits from recycling. Yet still, with the strong media and information campaigns, the notion of recycling finally became fashionable. Now almost every household in the Western world actively and responsibly recycles their garbage.

This recycling phenomenon is crucially important because it does not emanate from self-interest. It is a cause for the greater good that successfully changed the behaviour of billions of people.

This is the same mechanism that will bring an Open Economy, once it gets the sufficient desire of the people.

Bringing The Open Economy Today

Unlike recycling however, the change, this time, will probably not come from the leaders of the current system because they are too personally invested in it. Maybe that will change, but it's up to people like you and me, and the millions of others like us to show the others, and bring the Open Economy to everyone.

Now that the ideas of sharing and cooperation are already becoming viable alternatives to people, social media and the internet are already catching on. But the sharing needs to reach a critical 'threshold of usefulness' where it begins to challenge the existing market system. When that happens, it will become so popular that mainstream media will find it impossible to ignore. *That* is when the seismic shift will begin.

While a successful Open Economy requires the cooperation of everyone to create the desired abundance and diversity of skills, there are many ways we can manifest it today. By manifesting it today, we are not only moving away from the old systems, but we are learning and perfecting the new system while introducing it to others along the way. Here's the rundown of what you can do today.

Sharing!

Get into the habit of sharing your time, skills and resources with people you know. Look into sites like Freecycle, The Free World Network, Freegle, Streetbank, Timebanks, Hylo. All these sites allow you to search for and find useful items in your area to take or borrow, or free services offered by other people.

Community Sharing

Start or join a free sharing group in your area. There are many examples and templates you can follow. Check out the Community Sharing Circle idea on Freeworlder.com. For larger groups and villages, look into Ubuntu Contributionism.

If you have commercial space, a shop, or space available in a public area, consider setting up a 'Take It Or Leave It' stall or a 'Share Space', where people can take or leave something without payment.

Self Sufficiency

Becoming self-sufficient is a very attractive way of life and an act of rebellion to many people, but I should add a cautionary note: where we need to get to is a collaborative society. A self-sustaining life is a self-centred life, which is kind of the same mentality that has got us into the trouble we're in.

Anyway, that said, we do all need to learn more self-dependence and responsibility. Growing your own food is easy with a little patience – and, believe it or not, it comes right up out of the ground – free of charge! And when you have an abundance, you can share the fruits of your labour too!

Consider other ways to go self-sustaining as well, such as a solar water heater, rainwater trapping, using alternative fuel sources for your car or heating. Most of these cost money, but with a little ingenuity and some help from the internet, you can usually find low-cost or even free alternatives.

Educate Yourself!

Nowadays, there is almost no excuse for hiring someone to do something for you because you can learn it yourself! There is now a help and guide video for almost anything you need to do on YouTube or Wikihow. Everything from cutting hair to growing your own vegetables to fixing your car – all this information is now out there and has been provided free by volunteers! Learning a new skill is empowering.

Also, if you have a specific skill or something you could teach, then why not consider making a video and teaching others how to do it too?

Tool Libraries

Find a tool library in your area. If there isn't one, start one. These are a great way to share the tools and equipment that we rarely use. Because people already 'get' the idea of a library, it's easy for them to understand how it works and see the benefits.

Car–Pooling / Lift Sharing

This is not only a handy way for everyone to save cost for regular commutes but is also a good opportunity to discuss the underlying benefits and potential of an Open Economy with your driver or passenger.

Presumably, they will be sufficiently open-minded not to leave you on the side of the highway!

Use Open Source

Consider using open source software on your computer. This software is really advanced now. Linux and Ubuntu are powerful rivals to Windows; Open Office or Libre Office have all the same functionality of Microsoft Office, Word and Excel. Gimp is as good as or better than Photoshop. Audacity is a great audio recording tool, and VSDC is a powerful video editing package. These are just some examples. A quick search will reveal many more in your particular area of interest.

Build Your Own Home

Looking for a home? Consider a self-build eco home made from scrap or recycled materials. Again, thanks to the internet, there is a ton of information and guides out there now to help you build your own home from scratch. Generally, these eco homes also have a far higher degree of energy efficiency than regular houses and cost just a fraction of the price.

Of course, they can be labour intensive, but if you're committed or you have a lot of friends that can help you, then it's easy! Check out Earthships, Natural Homes and Open Source Ecology for some breathtaking inspiration. If you're thinking of embarking on a lifetime mortgage, don't!!

Become a Repair Guru

Re-learn the gentle art of repairing or repurposing your old or broken items. This was the normal practice for our parents' and grandparents' time, but plastic and disposable junk culture got in the way. Anything beyond repair can almost always be used for something else, so don't throw it away – be creative!

Repair Café

If you like repairing things, think of joining or setting up a repair café. These are proving quite popular now in Europe, and if you have a shop space you can set one up easily. The idea is that people come to get their stuff repaired while having a coffee and a chat. It's a great social initiative and, of course, payment is purely optional.

Go Vegan!

Not directly related to an Open Economy, but it is directly related to compassion, health and environmental issues.

Apart from sparing cruelty to animals, there is now overwhelming evidence that a plant-based diet is better for your body, and that livestock agriculture is one of the top contributors to climate change, both through methane emissions, and deforestation through forests being felled to make way for grazing.

There are also tons of great meat, milk and cheese alternatives available nowadays, so it's pretty easy!

Spread Awareness

Talk about your 'free' activities with people you know. Introduce them to the ideas of an Open Economy. Post on your social media pages about the ideas. Look at initiatives like The Free World Charter, The Zeitgeist Movement, The Venus Project, Ubuntu, New Earth Nation, The Money Free Party, Resource-Based Economy. There is a massive amount of material out there now to help you spread the message.

Promote This Book

I have intentionally made this book as short and simple as possible to try and reach more people with this message.

Please quote freely from this book, share it on your social media or pass it around to your friends. If you want, you can make reprints[10] and give them away or even sell copies to people in your area who you think are ready to hear this message.

This change starts with you and me, so let's begin?

The Open Economy

freeworlder.com/openeconomy

---

10   A reprint licence is available from the author. See inside front page.

Recommended Web Resources

www.freeworldcharter.org

www.freeworlder.com

www.thezeitgeistmovement.com

www.thevenusproject.com

www.newearthnation.org

www.ubuntuparty.org.za

Search YouTube For:

'make everything free'

'zeitgeist addendum'

'jacque fresco'

'contributionism'

'resource-based economy'

'peter joseph'

'alan watts'

'gift economy'

Other books from this author:

F-Day: The Second Dawn Of Man
Countdown to a moneyless world. The story of transition.

Lightning Source UK Ltd.
Milton Keynes UK
UKOW05f1825100317
296391UK00009B/70/P